PRESENT

TENSE

COMPLEX

PRESENT TENSE COMPLEX

Suphil
LEE PARK

CONDUIT BOOKS
& EPHEMERA

ISBN: 978-1-7336020-4-4

Published by Conduit Books & Ephemera
788 Osceola Avenue
Saint Paul, Minnesota 55105
www.conduit.org

Book design by Scott Bruno/b graphic design

Distributed by Small Press Distribution
www.spdbooks.org

Cover images courtesy the Library of Congress:
Lithograph by Adolf Giltsch after sketch by Ernst Haeckel;
Nest and eggs of ptarmigan, or Arctic grouse.
Humpback whale, ShutterStock.

CONTENTS

From the Waterfront the Horizon Always Is a You

the tongue of this impulse to race to rest

                                    —the torque

if every sun machetes one horizon   as every horizon

does one sun   if spirals spiral

into more spirals   in water set free

billows in earnest   set free

                  won't you stay

                        attuned for now

            you to whom this white land of lather

forays, spun undone, you from whom it thrashes back

I.

PRESENT:
현재/현재의, 존재하는, 선물, 보여주다

TENSE

COMPLEX

Weanlings

The whale was real.
> So was the beach, carsick
> & damp in the armpits as I was.
Father's shaggy hunk
> of leg against my young flank.
The crowd on the shoulder
> of the road watching the crowd
> smoke around the whale
I mistook for a stranded barrel.
> Did it outswell the ocean
> with breathing, was it yearling-
> white, bruised like light
> entering a dark room, in its lipless
> mouth an unlit cigarette
—you would never ask.
> Father took me to other beaches
after I kicked the whale
> in the flank and fell. The strangest I found
> beached there, threadbare underwear.
With a wick's lightness
> he'd shoulder me above
> the surface until no longer. I grew.
Hair & finger or toenails & memories too.
> With which to reshape me
> apart from age. Every scar a stamp
> that sends me back to where I ached.
I forget too easily what shaped each.

Wind-Borne Madness

Enter with your hiss-face.
Enter uprooted, unwholesome in rain.
Enter, buried in my dead friend's faux leather.
Enter with an armful of teeth dripping blood.
Enter, a bloodmist cashmere
of foraging ants in tow.
Enter through the keyhole
surgery to fix room temperature,
this December stale for years.
Enter, however easy it is to find home
in a body, though not every body's king's ransom.
Enter as empty-
handed as a domino builder
of burning candles, as a breeze
that arrives after years
of knocking curtains apart
through open windows across the world.
Enter here—where I'm reaching
for my grief as for a first lover's crotch.
Enter, rabid bird, for whom
the space under your feet
is one wave spreading
from one edge
of life to another—the bluer the ripple,
the deeper you burrow.

Sleeping through Wreckage

My pillow's a stethoscope.
                    Every night I hear you
sigh, on the other side of home-
                    sickness, louder and louder
until the night moves
                    to another generation.
Five flights ago you whispered
                    through a swarm of curls
at the funeral, no one
                    could prevent it—victims
returning to their memories.
                    When was the last time
you heard a nation
                    disappear under the wings
of an airplane, sky
                    the color of shipwreck.
Once in your mid-autumn
                    skin were too many names
of cities erased. Once in the ruins
                    of a childhood your mother
tongue turned rancid.

In the Head Full of Dead Letters

Borrowed light alone can't make out
this house I've never filled.
With your hands blinding me
I can finally see through your eyes.
Windowsills froth with baby's
breaths rearranged like a chain
of events in hindsight. Generations
of weathers have vined down
the outer wall as a candle loses light.
We lose life in unknowable increments.
How to account for this gravitation.
This longing to leave oneself behind.
A winter ago, a fisherman wanted you
to hold his hand while taking
last year's haul from the tide. He looks
so sad even now we cannot tell his age.
Closer, I'll say. For the night
in your eye is a shade colder.
How in this dark can we ever tell
where the perimeter of being starts.

Deluge

Let me be dramatic—to watch her emerge
as would a net full of thrashing fish
over the opaque surface of time.
The poem would have ended here
had dear Mr. Turtle not been dying
somewhere in the Pacific, since he drifted
from Hawaii, around his neck a thong I couldn't unknot.
To watch the day warm
between her striding bare thighs
unable to take lust seriously.
The whole beach, a pink wart. She has strolled
up from where water falls flat as if to die
to wake me up. *Marble pretends to worship your ankles*
just like the ocean, Achilles' mother must have said
seeing her child thud around soaking wet.
They all wanted him felled
in her eyes. But chance is no accident.
Emotion not an accumulation of images
but a wavelength from whose one end
each, alone, departs.
And her foal legs don't stretch across
the circumference of my future as she claims
the bed and suntan oil. I wouldn't be the doubt
cast on the promise
of perfect bikini lines, I swore
over god knows how many turtle eggs
buried on god knows how many shores.
Between the hatchlings
and water lurk so many dangers—were I Mother
Nature, when they begin to undulate
in a safe shade of blue, I would pull one end
of the ocean like covers, tuck those reptiles far away
from where she basks for long hours
of certain blisters. No one will come

to corner us into shelter. Nor will I come
back for her. Only one in a thousand
makes it to puberty.
The most we can say
of the past is that at least once, everyone died.
A demi-god would say, *Hope*
thus perseveres until the last one falls.
Snow is the year falling to its knees
before lifted into light. Or so
she believes. To weigh the light falling
around her like crinoline
as she slithers out of the garment
of her thoughts. *Walk up to me*
and fight face to face, Achilles said
in those preposterous sandals. Who's equipped
to confront the mortal's fear bare-handed, which billow
in the seascape of her emotion am I traveling.
The turtle will travel on, unable to locate
the cause of his short breath, as far as the simplicity
of longing doesn't wear him out.
She touches me where my pelvis threatens
to meet her palm, as if to challenge, *Who are you*
to ask for more. I am here to ask
if defiance is a virtue
even or only in the absence of gods.
The contrivance of mother-of-pearl across clouds
when a sun frowns. She unfolds
like afternoon. And I rewind, past the sand dunes
on fast forward, knowing many
have beat me to it.

In the Purgatory That This Brief Death Is

No one believes in free will—I'm telling you
with the itchy foot of a travelogue poem,
on the shore of August
and its amplified French kissing.
These waves racing after each other's tails
without means to grab, were they born
this way, or is it the wind.
A lap ahead my father goes rattling
his costly sorrow like ice cubes
in cognac, having never known
his mother, but what does it mean
to me as I toss mine
in the water after deeming it a drab detail
of no-stranger's life. At the end of life
someone's expecting each of us.
At the end of mine I imagine this girl I once loved
standing in a field of what's disguised
as blunt, blue flowers. They're destined to open
as I wade my way to her. Each flower a stranger's face
to which I'm impervious. It was a blunt, blue night
that I met each of them and forgot.
I'm destined to say, *The wind
has amounted to a direction, and I am
here, my past has amounted to the person
who's now crossing this field
of what I was free to choose to where you are
expecting someone likely not me,
but I am here with these details I am
to forget.* Then over her shoulder I see
a stretch of another field.
Another person waiting in it.

Herewith

It's settled you don't return.
The ocean rises, a giant
body of fur. However long
the route between a
you and the—I watch, watch,
watch. Watching is my gift.
It takes sheer will to give
my full attention. The gist
of spring in magnolias
maimed like heads
of young seals. *Wrath* misspelled
as *wreath* on sand as sounds
distract. A girl rises
from the trough
with a toy shovel as I watch
the girl turn the shovel up then
down elbow-deep in the throat
of water like Rhea a knife
short of insanity frisking
for god knows
and I do not know what.
I chose my lane
a highway ago. It took me
here, not there, and the water
now stays with me sane.

Victims

Every time she stews pork,
lard clouds the pot, peppers
over the broth like flies.
She remembers how dark
clouds descended—ground
alert—that summer
when the boys tore her
rabbit apart and left one
ear in the bloodstained grass.
The ear lay there, green
bean listening into the soil
for the body of its roots.
In downpour she held it close
to her face and read like a palm
reader each vein. Health
and wealth. An early
rebirth. Later she planted
the ear next to a white boulder.
It would grow a freight train,
a fountain, a fog of summer
insects over the years. Then
came the songs of a nascent
storm she now hears
stirring the pot, thinking,
no storm has found a way
to send an ocean down here.

To Side with the Bees

Honey, without the memory of a cloud
of bees near home, misses the longing
or what takes its place to make it sweet.
Adolescent pear trees abloom in pearly pus.
The orchard dressed
by the same fingers that will undress it
when each flower folds into a fist of possible life.
If we have an eye for stripes,
bees are fragmented gold in the dark.
Shards of shards, each aglint, like a child's muscle
memory—a matter of time in unsafe hands. *My mother-*
home, of course, my mother's home.
Easier to find a way home when it's necessary to sneak in.
Knocking without answer, what makes one
a more bitter child. Not let enter, answered.
Why hold this light of fragrance in the paper
bulb longer as if it matters. It matters.
Pruning of desire, perfect pleasure.
Beyond a thin thread of creek lie ancestral skeletons,
thousand-pointed teeth stained with mamushi tracks.

Pomegranate

A night of snow sits coiled
on the pine tree like a brain.
She wakes up with a litter
of thoughts to drown.
The pine shields her
barn when her patience
agitates the fogbound sun.
In her head she renders lighter
the night her daughter left
so she can see the tress
of her shadow leaving
—after which she blessed,
as does a woman at peace
with the world, some scarecrows
with fringes for the wind to twirl.
The unstoppable fact of hunger
has been so many's undoing.
She's fed the cows what the land
couldn't for two winters.
The fruit trees, repetition
of good weather and most
of her bad hours.
Waist-deep in snow, the pine
remembers the spring air
disturbed by nuptial flights,
her daughter a girl
who couldn't tell figs
from pomegranates.
The girl sat, mindless
of what the gaunt swing could stand,
mindless of the horsefly
that just dined on death, biting
into the purple flesh of a fig
after another, her teeth red like seeds

of another fruit.
The flat green before her
was alive with insects, each lifetime
a shivering stretch of gullet.
At night, the sun was nowhere
but underground.
Faithfully, each dawn,
her mother opened the curtains
for anything that stays
out of sight long enough
becomes a god.

Far Too Long Nothing Has Come

across rice paddies scythed
at the Achilles tendon

for a woman on the platform embracing
a bouquet of erigerons as if it's her past-
life child reborn at long last

to say, *I am the sentence*
you have to carry

through a slowing train
so the woman about to give up waiting
remains

ever in this form, as lightning travels
window after window each of which flashes
a different landscape

to cradle a crowd
of cut flowers in wax, lifting
their one waist

with bloody ankles, calling, *Mother, amulet*

are you here?

At 4 A.M. Snow

Fog is suddenly brought
over the river, the dead
having sighed on
their past in unison.
Earth stands on
end, listening.
The acid sun turns on
limes green as leaves
surrounding them.
Mother has planted
fruit trees on the verge
of discovering the river's
hackles are water's
bones. Father, upstream, ice
fishing. On and on.
Some morning coheres in frost.
In the shade of its coherence,
we can bear no one.

After Her Mother's Funeral Mother Calls Me into the Kitchen

Places my wrist next to the knife.
A growing mound of lemon slivers, celery green with wilting veins.
Time to feed myself first, she says, there's no shame in want.
My arms, first to go. Soft as eels bathing in whiskey.
Baby, Mother says lifting my leg, isn't it a boon to give.
Prying apart my lungs, I have put these
together, and am starving from separation.
Herbs soon overrun Mother, their names her only memory.
Lastly, rawly, my eyes to slurp.
The rest of my head folding in the fabrics
of my birthplace, ears against her ribs.
I will not give, Mother cries inside, birth to you this time.
Along with sadness she now carries my eggs.
My left eye sits on the windowsill, watching the last of me.
Mother drinking the right eye with frothy egg white.
Our dog lapping at bloodstains across the floor.
A hungry crow perching on the windowsill, its black eye
catching light in its black head.

Cost of Living

Understand my urge to make this
personal. Every death
without demur. I've watched
with my limbs planted
in vintage combat boots.
A frisson of daylight down the dark
well where Mother keeps
a dessert watermelon.
Daughter sits spooning it out
to a bloody helmet
before putting it over her head.

A Nestling's Mood of Disorientation

Your clan of cranes wants geraniums
one identical shade of garnet. Annually,

faithfully, breathable pageantry. You loved
nothing but loved to watch your aunt

dying. Her softening grip of reality.
As if capsized, hull forced into the cold
current, she was out of the blue beautiful.

No more cranes akimbo in the midst of poems
now barren of flowers as hardcore porn.

Still you keep an eye out for the foreshadowing
of their white wings against the floral gore.

That forethought like a doorknob you need to turn
before taking your sadness into another room.

Dye

In a menstrual cycle of balsamines
doubt revisits me.
The way it congealed
into the deer's face, eyes punctured
open by saber-toothed dread.
The balsam petal
paste on my fingernails
ages red as ruptured mouths.
There goes the green tail of August.
There goes, pollinated air.
There goes the scythe
of my mind straight into
cornstalks the height of the past.
My kitchen floor remembered
the deer shoulder you'd brought home
for three deaths in the family.
The meat, heft of gore and fur,
which my hands now seem
to have tusked through.
There goes the sun
that can't contain itself.
What kind of fear gave eyes
to the bat, only to blind.
What gave the spider four pairs.
The cornstalks billow in the rhythm
of knowing, not-knowing, between.
There goes my scythe, blade first.

II

PRESENT

TENSE:
경직된, 시제, 긴장시키다

COMPLEX

The Islet and Foreigners

You wanted to visit the piano museum
shelved on a cliff, preferring the climb
to its end. Stone steps meant for the cast
of *Black Swan*. The instruments expecting
willowy tiptoers with thumbs that fit
the thimbles of raspberries. I could show you
mine, knuckles still thick, two generations
after the last calligrapher. I showed you
where the sea thinned as my bloodline
after the IMF, seven kids per marriage
to two at best. *Which do you think is the sun
at its best—when rising or setting.*
You preferred its face half buried in water.
The islet out of breath in our wake.
The horizon, legs spread to the limit.
I needed some immediate pleasure rushing
to our rescue. Blame the flimsy rails. Blame
the bald spots on hills. Blame the ferry ride
that edged me like a raspberry on a fruit tart,
but those pianos were too young to be antique.
Youngest pines there, a century senior.
At least the pianos drowned out the silence
with an illusion of sound. You perhaps imagined
some D minor, a fugue, the kind Caesar
must have heard before the Rubicon.
I imagined a moon, full as the sun that ran out
of blood, lapping the doors of those European-
style houses. Eclipsed by the irrelevance
of paper lanterns. Tourists strung along.
Along the way we developed a taste for the civility
of not blaming each other at the dining tables.
Not when I ordered duck's head and grabbed one
by its beak. Not when I found contagious
your need to not see the face of your meat.

You preferred your duck reduced to a pink dollop
with figs and bread. I checked the cotton threads
of our covers for the week, that no window faced
west where each sun drowns, lest the dead
passed through your sleep. When you entered
the bed like a cold tongue, I made you first meet
the need of my face. It was an important trip,
you see.

Complicit in Now

By which point in life do we become water-damaged
water bottles. All save those who kept life, like a vase,
at arm's length. Simple took mindless amens, an osmosis
of bucket list wishes, a safe distance from the frivolous,
frantic, free to fret over the *f* words. Keep us alive, fate.
In the business of imagination we see the red wax seal
in place of a mouth. Feel the urge to undo the envelope
of scalp: shouldn't there be more behind that face of yours,
a letter or an initial addressing a you. Even buttons needed
to be invented. Someone must have cared dearly if not
you, for this fully imagined humanness to be ours.

　　　　　　　　　What a relief—to accept
this ready-made world. To accept the knowledge
preceding our knowing: the heart we find against all odds
writhing—mother hosing down our home with blood
as a reminder that war wants us, and wants us to believe
it never is here. All save darkness have their feet on
a false bottom, unable to reach the bottom of darkness.
Fathom this: what made us will single-handedly undo us.
Fathom this: we come undone before we get unmade.
In the business...What doesn't dim, wane over time.
　　　　　We are made of nothing but reflections.

On the Way Home

A girl jogs past me, an earphone cord swinging
loose like a string of her brain. She's a song
buzzing by, with my eyes shut. Thick with snow
is the park, save the path in the making, gray
under a stray dog's paws. What for dinner,
what for. Unleashed dogs sniff out next pit stops
in the November slush. What for. Did the girl ever fall
for someone who clapped open bottled sauces
without spilling like her father. Kids chatter
away, tongues gauzed with bubble gums as if
each growing a gator's egg-tooth in the throat.
About to hatch. Impending about. I feel some death
like the promise of my mother's. Numerous people
jumped to their deaths. A thousand-chopstick-
long flight off that building. Numerous heaps
of canned food thumped onto plates around the city.
It's hard to differentiate—this archive in disarray.
In the commuter belt wind brushes the reeds.
All of them on the rebound, elastic as muscle.
Ready to fling back into place, then out again
and again. Life will grow deaths out and outgrow
the rest it hasn't. Another afternoon of snow
will bury the dog's path, but you are now
                                        on your way.

Dusk

Desire is liquid, inside or out. I tell you in this dream where we sleep together, once a month. Shapes of erection whet the wind. Skyscrapers, spires, traffic poles. All against a sky pigeon-breasted with clouds. The clouds copulate in rain, shapeless, finding opening in earth. While we listen, holding each other close.

You've been looking for a job to afford a room with two windows facing each other. Like this very room we're very sad in. A perfect symmetry, reflecting the asymmetry of what happens to it. You're no longer a girl ripping apart a dead pigeon to see what fills its chest. Wouldn't it be nice to have a reminder, you ask, that day and night share one slab of sky.

Our government's cartographers mapped the pine belts, mushroom belts, the belts of reproductive women. *Light,* the noun, is here to unlatch the grip of fog that commands the road leading out of this dream. We're numbered. Take them off, you say, one by one. Your socks, your days.

I'm where habit predicted. Life, a square I can put on a spoon but can't unfold. I climb a mountain to meet the mountain in person. Its torso, cyanide-blue. Rashes of autumn. Walking down the trail I took up, I finally understand the feeling of the season. All that left will return likewise, stamping wisteria petals on the road it sped down. I turn to you, folded, naked, to understand how I feel. In this square room in this square dream.

Low to the floor you are, like a nocturnal animal alert with thirst. Your head an exact weight of heat in my lap. The rest of you disappears. Trees imitating the blue pulse of the ocean over dead cicadas. We're two-thirds liquid. Does it mean we're two-thirds desire. Are we palpitations mostly. I turn to you. The fleet of your teeth prison windows. Light's lisp.

I give you this weightless form of meaning. The shoes you take off disappear into the depths of the room. They mean nothing without the sound of them hitting the floor. The floor means nothing without the shoes meeting it. Pries open this dream. What keeps it upholstered apart from all this wetness. How the exact weight of an emotion is measured in the lack of it, later.

Down the lane of fog, an island of headlights comes floating. We watch it fill the room with fluorescence, and a dish of salted mushrooms with the appetite of moist. Out of touch with desire, are we one-third of our self. The thought seizes my throat, like seawater, which in dark, raiding swirls, pushes around a woman on a styrofoam raft. She's numbered. To the better-sunned regions of your skin, your freckles have migrated. Seize me here. Where the therapy of talking fails, we make a cloister.

Compatriot Ballad

Remember the clouds near the ground like gurneys
looking for the aftermath of war, centuries later.
There's nothing left to lift
but the barley in a good streak.
Where the soldiers fell
a four-way road now runs and a bakery
wafts a tradition of red beans.
One might say back in the day death was simpler.
Or the women teetered with reed baskets
atop their heads. Their children, elliptical, some shorter
than rifles, cropped up everywhere.
Daggers poured from the sky, the history
turned folklore might say in a thousand years,
when an old woman teaches her grandson to garnish
each bread with the glaze of a golden Buddha
beheaded by walls of incense.
Some of the smoke leaves in one piece like a road.
The dead leave the temple in peace through paper doors.
Remember the grandson on the brink of mile
after mile of reed, barley, and beans.
He lifts his hand to deflect the wind
that sweeps over the land, making its eyes
with lashes of pistils blink.
The sun has a finger pointing out his thirst.

Song of No Trust

On the outskirts of a war
your baby teeth were baptized
cities which kneaded
eclectic sorrow into light.
Everything lying on your green
tongue—the damp night
nothing but a mouth, much to devour.
Lamplights couldn't find
the knolls of cut ears
in the folds of a century past,
couldn't wage water
going still in the lap
of a cross-legged lake.
No grasshopper leaps
from the grass when the past
trudges through and back.
Afraid of heights in secret
the insects learned to leopard-crawl.
Was it not a favor for nature
to rip the legs off. Is it not human
nature to embrace the fervor
for conquest, or like a colony
of bees, to write the color of threat
in our bone marrow.
Out of love you understated the memory
of permanent teeth or lack thereof.
The entire field quiets
green as soldiers in wait.
Some past preserves the present tense.
What does it, then, now
mean: out of love. How much of kindness
comes from contempt. How much
of it habit. How much, young
earth, for yours.

At This Hour of Long Sky

You dawn. See across.
Not an elongated road ahead
and behind. Not its intestine
across the foggy swamps
closing in on me. *I* happens
when a mythical creature adopts
a familiar face. The devil perhaps
is a girl with poor pigtails.
Upturned, anything
can resemble a pair of horns.
She suckles one prawn's head
after another, tasting sulfur in salt.
The sheer desire for life
holds the apparatus of life together.
Does she feel it at work,
this age of fog turning
into a mind-threatening city
empty but for her, all grown-up
and in all black, lighting
a cigarette for a wax-white
man in a wheelchair, his IV drip
invading the dark like a lanterned kite
while I, without feeling, think
how my mother tongue
pronounces IV the way I do *linger*.
The hospital where their loved one
is dying is not here.
But the light's eloquence travels—feeling
nothing accentuated
unjustly, no war in proximity,
which makes the rest of the night easier
when *I* is but a button
holding down a blue, diverging ripple
of time about to burst

into its true form—a single color
where I'm adrift
without drifting in the least.

Tug of War

1.
By a few ropes of light
the world is hanging like an idea
of home. In its foyer I listen
to the rain's dark veins.
In a back room, wars rage.

2.
I whisper *unleash
light,* you hear *end is lie.*
Ringworms of poppies spread
as you grind every morning
an apple to shreds of flavor.
If I returned
branches to this wooden chair,
would it return to a sapling.

3.
Some dictators amputated—
down to the marrow of humanness.
An eyeball in a jar, gray matter.
Or misheard last words, "bury me
in your orchard" (so I can poison
your apple's thirsty thoughts),
that could've been "buy me
an orchestra," through bloody teeth.
What willed an orchestra to continue
to play on a sinking ship can sink
its teeth in us. Unleash
light. As I hug your head
so tight it shakes in my ribcage.

4.
When I go numb
thumb my hand this way.

5.

Kelp forest between thighs of land.
Continent of a cattle herd.
Child slapping her itchy scars to sleep
in the floe-green field. Glowworms
filling the summer's mouth like a denture.
A distance between all this
and you is the distance between a tree
and unvarnished wood. Draw your chair
to this window. Would I ever be a single thought
to break a mind's surface.
Even my dread is not pure.

6.

In the thick of benevolence, if you returned
sleep to me, would I become
more or less.

7.

Every human narrowed down
to a few blunders.
The moon, a well's mouth.
Every sun a bucket
that breaks each night's surface.
Beginning handcuffed
to end. The one in control
to what's on his leash.
Guided by a few ropes of light
we dread on.

8.

Here comes another day
set out to retrieve the ropes
pulled taut by unremarkable hope.

Tidal Migration

She waned in the neighborhood of my first love, like sounds that turn
mute in another language. My oblivion was not a sign of innocence. I
misplaced Rs often and relied on Ls as on a longer front tooth. Listen. Look.
Let me explain. In my memory, faces kept eroding, became cubist or lost
a nose, a mouth. Hate drove her to invisibility. Some mornings, I'd still
find my toothbrush wet. At night, her fingerprints on the pane of gelatin
darkness. Forgotten faces were reduced to vestigial pools that reflected
my own. Through their wet pores I could breathe. Each night was a cube,
rearranged once I entered. She was a tongue stiff as a dictator one moment,
a transparent peninsula with umbilical coordinates the next: *Look
how the lights got the tennis elbow from battling with night
after night, this toned streetlight—*
When words were too heavy, I'd cup her with my hands.
Some of her dripped on my way to bed.

Venus Tongue

In a nutshell: to think

on one axis becomes religious.

Who dares to climb one's family tree.

Who named flowers before language.

Listen to her breathe on the turf of froth:

    Farewell, far-flung pollens

    of hunger, this

    life   at famine price. Farewell, no

    end in sight.

She'll name it—Absalom

Quo Vadis   Simon   sallow rose

rustling awake from its fractured skull.

She'll name it

        find-me:

    Find me   with the urgency of field

                          dressing.

    Find me   on the horizon

           inching towards the sky bending

    into a globe.

Then find me   again

        out of breath on this upside-down

                fiddleback tree, again

           on the cusp of armlessly falling.

Subtraction

This is my temporary mind.

Stated thoughts,

                black roses.

(I often write you out, then into

                my mind.)

To verify this I have pictures

hung upside down: your lips

a flat line in conflict, clothesline

                pulled taut by lightness.

I write   from this mind.

You taught me math

in color: "Red + Blue = Purple."

Imagination is an intraocular organ.

Night

an intrinsic factor in the sun

                that converges to light.

A secret, an unstated fact.

An equation of vacuum lies

                between 59

                and 60,

                11.8 and 12, night

and midnight.

I write *you,* for you

aren't my secret.

Instead I wear you

like spectacles, refuse to blink.

Math in image: "Rain + Sun = Rainbow."

To which I asked, "Sun = Bow?"

You answered, "Sun = Rain (Bow-1)."

This is my mind, analogous to a hat

that swallows my face but declines the name

mask. Emptied, it lies flat

like a bag.

Mind, name. What is shared

cannot be secret.

In my mother tongue I say *our*

           mother, to any of *you*

           I've never met.

Our home, which I alone occupy.

If We = You + I, but We = I,

you is 0, pure

        as it disappears.

Imagine: black roses

curled up in the lifeform of their deaths.

If the eye is the destination—

                from the mind

—night diverges, becomes

                light, vice versa.

No space is empty, unless emptied.

I want this space

                between roses and the wind

to close.   In time.

Imagine: the sun arching

                to its limit,

a blister of light   to share.

The arrow, gone.

Tired of My Voice, I Speak in Flames

Mother says no one can tame
blisters, tugging at my tongue.
Nightly the fridge houses
my head to slow the brain
melting neuron by neuron, wax
of thoughts flooding
my mouth—liquid vowels pooling
up from the swollen toes, up
my spinal cord, purple
ripples of tart words climbing
up, past the floodline between the first
rib and shoulder blades.
So this is how you set yourself on fire,
teeth bloody with ashes. Everything leaves
my pustulous mind wet
as sex. Now I see it—the relationship
between life and living is like that
between pain and suffering.
Everyone I map out in ink burns
like my body. They all know death
in and out, they know it
intimately.

Itinerary of Speech

I am rooted, but I flow.
—Virginia Woolf

The tree warped by wind is made
of wood, despite another tongue
in mind. Across the river, afraid
of touch like unexfoliated elbows,
egrets. Everything they love folds
into one mouthful. So does what
I love, nestled between molars.
The horizon is locked in the denture
of space bisected by the teeth
of our eyes. Sunset a scar outgrowing
its share of scars. The misshapen tree
that rattles its shadow on windless days
is made of wood, still. There's nothing
sad in the tree's script about genitalia
save our attachment. Or about
the waterborne moon that brings
to mind a milk tooth or the kneecap
of a drowning woman, rapids
fiddling with the strings of her hair,
as would a breeze. The tree will
continue to lose its voice by the volume
of leaves shed. Skulls, teeth.

Hung in Her Persimmon Tree Is Night's Wolfskin

Crows are pecking it apart to white lies.
A sun exits her lair. She's been marked
with liver spots where moons were cut
from her skin. The crows cry in a pack,
shadowing her land's slow darkness.
She's alone. Persimmons shrink
into a hopeless shade of phlegm.
The wind mistakes them for the heads
of hanged thieves and leaves shaking.
Stay for the night, she tells anyone
passing, in the bowel of our silence
we'll be overwritten as water and its instinct
to meet to leave. The ripe persimmons falling
to turn her yard into a slaughterhouse floor
are symbols. Her face, another that details
time. Seeing an ant shoulder an insect
leg three times its size like a cross, she rushes
to step on it. Just as women sun-bitten
in the faces belong to her, the ant belongs
to the night that keeps one starving
for another body to outweigh the nearing
death. Near truth, life is but a symbol.
She wishes not to speak of solitude tonight.
The world seems to float in the quietude
of being frail—many details stolen overnight.
It is the same world. Even as the ant rolls out
of her light unscathed, then away, a drop of ink.

This Is the Only Way to Speak

A gust of snow slits
ajar a mouth among branches.

       I have an island to keep blank.

Waves rave ashore
slowing around a deserted island
protectively.

       Run down those flights of stairs.

Beyond the horizon is another night in flight
from its fixated existence.

       I needed you
       to gut me so you could narrow
       me down like a fish.

Beyond the horizon is what meets the line's both ends.
Its circumference, the island, empty, shoulders.
Is it not easy to forget the weight
when snow keeps falling in flecks.

       I have an island made of water.

Let the wind through, let it phrase
what's next to shudder.

III

PRESENT

TENSE

COMPLEX:
복잡한, 단지, 강박관

Friend, Whatever You're Thinking

You're thinking it into a frown.
Let's not near that leading edge
of sorrow you frequent. Desire,
god, blesses you, with the urge
to live or to stop. This is a world
before the invincible roaches
make divine landfall and conquer.
To this I'm attached, for now.
Easy pleasure of entrusting our brain
to lateral thinking. Utility poles
we can court drunk or not. Growing out
of bad habits into others. That one
mysterious thing that's always elsewhere
we think will prompt us home
as a wartime curfew. The law
of averages: there comes someone
across a foreseeable future's distance
who will hang you between two
poles—of desire to save, or to flee
—someone who will arrest you
like a newborn's eye looking out
from between her mother's legs.

Against Botany

Perhaps every poet should take to a garden.
I prefer a yard, and one in abandonment.
Oblique cinquefoils spilling into thickets
like drunk college girls, no elsewhere
left to turn to. Palm prints of soil all over
day-old stems. More dirt than anything,
most die out fast. But always more to fill in.
Play the scene at the speed of reminiscing,
and it'd be flashbacks of an entire meadow.
There's no relevance, preference, or order
in sprouting, just the fact of its persistence—
even as the old apricot tree blooms furiously,
only to forsake its flowers like lice, fruitless,
the yard stunned by accidental flowers each
time, no blueprint in mind, this keeps rolling on
in all the mud. What it'd be like to rise from
the rotting flesh of their own kind, how much
more than a pure instinct I'd need to collect
just to consider it, I can't begin to imagine.
Even poppies ambush some winters, meaning
no harm. They have no way to tell what they are
or the threats of their mere appearance. I don't mind
watching them without thinking. Don't mind
their absence of intention taking up the shape
of greed—redder, brighter, more conspicuous
by dawn. Don't mind how loud. Or how their mind
never comes near why I am there all along.

In the Grand Scheme of Themes

The poet instills an ocean in each line to push back the horizon.

Dear gambling brother, she writes, a throng of harpooned whales

will surface, each reef-crowned. Bomblets of limpets, upstairs

that dovetail all floors, high-rises with glass ceilings—we replicate

so much. We can't help ourselves or our motherland corseted

in party lines. I know nothing of love, she says, but it's become

a language of loss here. Empty structures we build without are filled

with the sounds of tapping us out, our tapping into each other's mind.

So many reasons there are to question the ocean, it's become invisible,

genetic. A tautology over the horizon's mane. The poet sneaks a comma

on a line's head before wading in, out, until she lucks out. Enters at dusk

a bat cave where a wave of darkness simulates another, in the dark aflicker.

Another Day Dead from Having Been Awake Too Long

What bees had in mind for home
resembled a magnified eye
of a fly, a globe full of holes.
What made their colony a hive of hexagons.
The gravity that whisks life askew.

Death amortized by the hours spent asleep.
An addled, collective mind cavorts
in a mobius strip. A bee's eye view
grasps first what it starves for—colors
before the contours of flowers.

Where the cliff folds like a kick pleat
desire remains accessory to imagination.
Night releases spores through which
some greater relief promises to arrive.
Can hornets stomach the gall to die.
Will spring relent ever.

Worker bees strip off the darkness
of bellflowers they entered like small suns.
Sometimes, sometimes, they chant.
Everything can fit into the small room
of sometimes, can it not.

Inconsequential Is the Name of Everything

through the spokes
> of sunrise a sun rises
hollered at centuries
> long—stride over, frayed
mind, in 9 P.M. light
> —eventful pores we are
what else are we
> something like bed
inchoate in daylight
> (against) what's outside
growing softer
> (sandpaper) and softer still

On a Scale of Nothing to All

Part of childhood remains
buried under sandcastles.
You used to poach
grasshoppers with an old hairnet
until it caught strands
of cobwebs and would not let go.
Memories are but hearsay.
So is a sachet that used to contain
scented soaps. So is
every emotion, even your own.
Only by intuition you know anger,
awake, splinters like sleep's
exoskeletons in the morning.
Under your window
spiderlings fiddle down
a rose stem after rain, so much at stake.
There you stand
lobbing a tennis ball, as sure
of gravity as of dusk
that shivers inshore, searching
for a glade to fathom
the rest of the forest against.

In Short

You placed in each little egg a tumor
of emotion that the hatchling grows to embody.
I know the drill: collateral, colossal, sorrow unrelated
to a great cause always saving grace
somehow, deadpan beds and dining tables.
Greed's featherbone dense with weight.
Compassion flickers past like the diphthong in mail.
Most flightless, these birds end up in a cornering skid.
Roses grimace. For the beak of hubris is hunger.
For the beak of curiosity fits any vase with a flamingo's neck.
I leave fledgling appetite in the oven for midnight gloom.
Contempt knows the spectator's glee, knows our hearts
are poached just as our hard-shelled planet.
It would leak if pecked at enough. Every egg's teething
troubles—what to say about them
but the fledgling midnight looms,
a siege of farce will flock in terse snow.

Flight into Focus

Touch the muscled arm
of this manured field.

Extraneous
beauty emerges. Why
afraid.

Even a hummingbird's wingspan
can tussle with the sky.

Houses sing
in a distance of sleep.

An inside-out sea
urchin is a mind opening
like a sky.

Off the future canters
in pink fur slippers.

My bones are never hollow
of oceanic grief.

Waterscape with No Heaven in Sight

Be tender with the future like a pair
of legs wading through a strange mind.

Islands and oases both Xs on its map.
Twisted driftwoods hem every X's rim.

Our movement scented by water reshapes
the water in our wake, not leaving a mark.

Heaven singing at the heart of hell—wait
with me, hand in hand.

What is your hand has each finger
                    named, same as mine.

Should You Wade

In this water convulsing incandescent
        with jellyfish, be on guard.
Your childhood violin resurfaces
        as a gutted fish. Its fiddle suffered
at your hands and is now an amputated mast.
        Who blitzed the moon to syllables
in the ocean where morning never existed.
        Light has been the backbone to the meat
of darkness, as death to the self.
        A butcher's knife spills in tuna
its red memory. A conductor spills a second
        of silence before his arm drops.
Hopes drop, kept high during the day.
        God dumped noctilucent paint #innumerable
here before returning to his loveseat at Orion.
        Nestlings cry unafraid, their god being hunger.
In the vicinity of faith, someone needs to stand up.
        I've been standing all along, like a fish
caught then released into a fear of air.
        Do you understand the hunger of dark water—
pressure without teeth. Do you understand the fish,
        swimming away, unstrung and out of tune.
Rigidity becomes your posture after enough fear.
        Your memory, after enough standing.
God's nodding off amidst the molars
        of celestial light. Fold my mother's life
at the pelvis, and it'll become his knife.
        Moving from hers to his, I briefly was you.
Name your past, castaway, and I'll find the estuary
        to your hunger where a crane stands priestly,
steadying the first catch of dawn in his beak.
        The fish looks up at a crescent gill in the sky.

At a Stretch

It takes nothing to kill a snail.
Nothing to smear a snowflake dry
and nothing to neglect a newborn.
Bees swarm a globe of their own
nonetheless. A besieged egg.
It takes nothing to overlook their place
in the grand scheme of things.
Clouds congregate in one place
looking for their misplaced trunk.
Trees imitate the shape of weather.
It takes nothing to tell them apart
and nothing to look away from a storm.
A tantony pig left to die by his mother
sniffs out an approaching bucket
full of food. It takes nothing to lift him
off the ground, but nothing for rain
to pelt him to death. Undermine as you will
the time it takes to make a sandwich
from wheat seeds or the distance
cocoa powder travelled to arrive
in your mug. You put on your pants
and run along a fence without effort.
Colors are the first sign of wilting
and of swelling that you hardly notice
running, a month older each passing post.
Every herd has some that were the smallest
of their litter. Every herd, a black sheep.
Bees too soon out of hibernation go
steal from their neighbors. You share
your ice cream cone with your first friend.
Put as much distance between yourself
and the last war until you're in bed
with a lover. It takes nothing for things to align
sometimes. Nothing to blow off candles

in your head all at once but a kiss.
But it takes nothing to mistake a woman
bending before entering a new world
for kneeling to pray. A door doesn't grow
for passersby. It takes nothing to blame
the itinerary and to say everything ends
with a taut heart. But it takes nothing to start
and start again. At the heart of a cannonade
are those firing and those rushing to danger
to stop the bleeding with field dressings.
A stag beetle tosses another off the tree
that underground makes room for its brother's
roots to stretch. An ant alerts its colony
to a lifetime's worth of food, foreseeing
a collective future, not only its own.
Pain is to hope what fear is to life.
But it takes nothing to close your eyes.
Nothing to look in your galoshes across
the billows of land and to not think
how the earthworms' self-serving lives
improved your breakfast toast
whose breadcrumbs your daughter uses
to spell out her name, one letter wrong.
It takes nothing to confuse a snail
with a whisper of grass in the wet meadow.
Nothing to stand against a fencepost swaying
over the memory of holding a fetus-
looking piglet. It takes nothing to hold god
accountable. Life's been more than a mile
of pouring and yours, just one of billions.
There are many meadows beyond this one.
It is neither spring nor winter.
Now is but a particular temperature of light
by which you discern the past calmly

like the palm of your hand.
It takes nothing to save the dying pig.
Nothing to note the clockwork
of a throbbing heart that condemns
the hot-blooded this kinship in the cold.
Rain turns metaphorical with you
unshielded in a sentence, symbolic
with a lioness wandering a dry water hole,
belly ripped open like a drawer.
To the pig, rain is just an unfortunate
circumstance. To you, a reason to run.
Land isn't easily moved—the more
important job being holding itself together.
But it takes no more than hours of rain
for the land to expose its red mud
and to splatter anyone passing through it,
no more than you crossing the meadow
as would the animal tucked inside
your shirt, killing or scaring into flight
a thousand tiny insects, with whose eyes
the land springs to life, finally
to see its full expanse.

Hua Tou

Even though the great ocean should change,
it can never be communicated to you.

—Nansen

The syntax of youth is to age
unfazed. Young, big statements
mistake a period for the beginning
of ellipsis I vowed against....
Everything comes down to the turf
fight of second thoughts.
Where every word, wanting
its renewed reality, is always day-old.
Where I encounter death, for me,
waiting in my childhood
dog's grave.
Where the idea of home
is an index thinking up
the first draft of a book to house it.
Based on one sentiment
I've desired—I want you
at an insurmountable distance
for my life to go on
towards you.
A different stretch of despite
and because to swim across
lies between any two
of us. Up close, pain
has a lion's share in everything
we deem enduring.
But how short-lipped, the promise
never to name a pain.
Despite the desperation
of nouns, articles
choose to celebrate.
Because the pain

is a pain just as a pain
is the pain. A daily sequence
of sunlight is all it takes.
Even the darkest night.
Even the end of it.

PRESENT
현재/현재의, 존재하는, 선물, 보여주다

TENSE
경직된, 시제, 긴장시키다

COMPLEX
복잡한, 단지, 강박관념

현재 경직되고 복잡한
현재 경직된 단지
현재 경직된 강박관념
현재 시제 복잡한
현재 시제 단지
현재 시제 강박관념
현재 긴장시키다 복잡한
현재 긴장시키다 단지
현재 긴장시키다
강박관념을
현재의 경직되고 복잡한
현재의경직된 단지
현재의 경직된 강박관념
현재의 시제 복잡한
현재의 시제 단지
현재의 시제 강박관념
현재의 긴장시키다 복잡한

현재의 긴장시키다 단지
현재의 긴장시키다
강박관념을
존재하는 경직되고 복잡한
존재하는경직된 단지
존재하는 경직된 강박관념
존재하는 시제 복잡한
존재하는 시제 단지
존재하는 시제 강박관념
존재하는 긴장시키다
복잡한
존재하는 긴장시키다 단지
존재하는 긴장시키다
강박관념을
선물 경직되고 복잡한
선물 경직된 단지
선물 경직된 강박관념

선물 시제 복잡한
선물 시제 단지
선물 시제 강박관념
선물 긴장시키다 복잡한
선물 긴장시키다 단지
선물 긴장시키다
강박관념을
보여주다 경직되고 복잡한
보여주다 경직된 단지
보여주다 경직된 강박관념
보여주다 시제 복잡한
보여주다 시제 단지
보여주다 시제 강박관념
보여주다 긴장시키다
복잡한
보여주다 긴장시키다 단지
보여주다 긴장시키다
강박관념

ACKNOWLEDGMENTS

Thank you to the editors and staff of the following publications for providing homes to earlier versions of these poems, some under different titles.

32 Poems: "In the Head Full of Dead Letters"
Barrow Street: "The Islet and Foreigners"
Bennington Review: "In Short"
Birdfeast: "Far Too Long Nothing Has Come"
Colorado Review: "Sleeping through Wreckage," "Victims"
The Common: "Hua Tou"
diode: "Inconsequential Is the Name of Everything," "Itinerary of Speech"
Foundry: "Herewith"
Image: "At 4 A.M. Snow"
The Journal: "At This Hour of Long Sky"
jubilat: "From the Waterfront the Horizon Always Is a You"
The Malahat Review: "After Her Mother's Funeral Mother Calls Me
    into the Kitchen"
The Margins: "Tidal Migration"
The Missouri Review Online: "Friend, Whatever You're Thinking"
New South: "A Nestling's Mood of Disorientation"
Notre Dame Review: "Compatriot Ballad," "Song of No Trust"
Ploughshares: "Weanlings"
Poet Lore: "Against Botany," "In the Purgatory that This Brief Death Is"
Quarterly West: "Subtraction"
Salamander: "On a Scale of Nothing to All"
The Southeast Review: "Another Day Dead from Having Been Awake
    Too Long"
Sugar House Review: "Cost of Living," "On the Way Home"
The Summerset Review: "Flight into Focus"

"Dye" was shortlisted for the 2020 Montreal International Poetry Prize and anthologized in the *Global Poetry Anthology*.

"Against Botany" is for Loan Tran
"At a Stretch" is for Daniel Ruiz
"Compatriot Ballad" is for Shangyang Fang
"Friend, Whatever You're Thinking" is for Yuki Tanaka

ABOUT THE AUTHOR

Suphil Lee Park spent 9/14 of her life all over the Korean peninsula before landing in the American Northeast. Her name 수필 리 박 (秀筆 李 朴) consists of Chinese characters, each of which means "outstanding," "writing brush," "plum tree," and "silver magnolia." She graduated from New York University with a BA in English and from the University of Texas at Austin with an MFA in Poetry. Her poems and short stories appear in *Colorado Review, Global Poetry Anthology, Image, Ploughshares, Quarterly West,* the *Iowa Review,* and the *Massachusetts Review,* among many others. She's a literary agent who champions contemporary Korean writers. You can find more about her at www.suphil-lee-park.com.

CONDUIT BOOKS
& EPHEMERA

OTHER TITLES FROM CONDUIT BOOKS & EPHEMERA

Sacrificial Metal by Esther Lee

The Miraculous, Sometimes by Meg Shevenock

The Last Note Becomes Its Listener by Jeffrey Morgan

Animul/Flame by Michelle Lewis